Out of Words

31 Prayers of Hope for Your Hurting Heart

CARMEN HORNE

Out of Words: 31 Prayers of Hope for Your Hurting Heart

© Carmen Horne 2019
All rights reserved.

www.CarmenHorne.com

ISBN: book 978-1-7332627-0-5
ISBN: ebook 978-1-7332627-1-2

Published by: Carmen Trichell Horne

Cover and interior design by Jana Kennedy Spicer, Sweet To The Soul Ministries
Carmen's Photo by Misti Mixon Stone
Carmen's Makeup by Makeup by Olivia – Olivia Kemp

Unless otherwise indicated, all Scripture quotations are taken from the Holy Bible, New Living Translation, copyright © 1996, 2004, 2015 by Tyndale House Foundation. Used by permission of Tyndale House Publishers, Inc., Carol Stream, Illinois 60188. All rights reserved.

Scripture quotations identified as MSG are from *The Message*. Scripture taken from *The Message*. Copyright © 1993, 1994, 1995, 1996, 2000, 2001, 2002. Used by permission of NavPress Publishing Group.

Scripture quotations marked (ESV) are from The ESV® Bible (The Holy Bible, English Standard Version®), copyright © 2001 by Crossway, a publishing ministry of Good News Publishers. Used by permission. All rights reserved.

Scripture quotations marked (NIV) are taken from the Holy Bible, New International Version®, NIV®. Copyright © 1973, 1978, 1984, 2011 by Biblica, Inc.™ Used by permission of Zondervan. All rights reserved worldwide. www.zondervan.com The "NIV" and "New International Version" are trademarks registered in the United States Patent and Trademark Office by Biblica, Inc.

Endorsements

We all face times in our lives when we truly are "out of words," not knowing how to express our thoughts or whisper a prayer. This wonderful book provides a much-needed tool to help us navigate through those times.

On the pages of *Out of Words - 31 prayers of Hope for Your Hurting Heart* one can find wise words of instruction, daily prayers to guide us when we can't find the words ourselves, challenges, affirmations and hope-filled declarations based from the truths and promises of God's word.

I'm grateful to Carmen Horne for providing this book to guide us toward healing no matter the cause of our hurts. It is one I will refer to often and share with others in their time of need.

Cindy Cameron
Grief Support Group Facilitator
Director of JPC Foundation

WOW! This is a work of compassion, confession, and coaching from an authentic warrior that encourages and leads the reader to a place of hope and healing. Each nugget of life is a bitesize treasure that gently guides and speaks life into the one blessed to journey through the pages of this book. Mighty is the work this book will accomplish in the lives of its readers.

Dr. Veronica Sites
Crisis Response Chaplain
Founder at VS of Life

Has the unexpected left you breathless? Shattered? Scattered? Has your serenity surrendered or been swept away as grief grips your heart and growls at you? Are you so broken you are out of words, struggling even to pray?

Author Carmen Horne writes, "I'm convinced the prayers God understands most clearly are the tears streaming down our cheeks." Having buried a son and a sister, I agree.

Expect the Spirit to waft into your world through her words. How so? Carmen Horne points us straight to the Word of God, His Son, Jesus, in such a touching way, only God can be her source of words.

Choose to peer through, as Horne writes, "the binoculars of faith." I'm convinced God breathed His words through her for you and me to have the Word revived in us, renewing a bright hope for our future.

Get your copy of *Out of Words: 31 Prayers of Hope for Your Hurting Heart* now.

Dr. Susan B. Mead, Th.D.
Award-winning author and Founder of His Girls Gather

Carmen Horne has written an excellent book that will provide support, direction, encouragement, and hope to those who have experienced the overwhelming battles of life. If your life has not turned out the way you expected, with twists and turns and sorrow, this book is for you. It's a great combination of support and "how-to" that is so needed. This book will be on my recommended reading list for many of my clients!

Gil Martin
Licensed Professional Counselor
Marriage Coach for the Smalley Institute

I have had the honor and pleasure of knowing Carmen Horne for many years now. It's very rare that she is out of words! The one time she was without, Carmen was going through a season of great grief. She knows and understands our broken hearts and pain because she has lived it.

Carmen walks with us through our brokenness. She provides words when we have none of our own, comforting words from The Word.

As you read *Out of Words*, know this: every devotion you read, every prayer you pray, and every journal prompt you can't write because of your emptiness, will bring you closer to Jesus. He will fill you. Your words will return!

Ellen Chauvin
Writer at EllenChauvin.com, author of *Abiding Joy-Pondering the birth of Jesus*, and Bible teacher.

It is with much delight that I endorse *Out of Words: 31 Prayers of Hope for Your Hurting Heart* by Carmen Horne, Hope Coach. If you have ever suffered from a broken heart, then you know that grief is a personal and difficult process. After losing my brother in a tragic car accident, I struggled to find light in the darkness. However, after seeking God's Word, I returned to the affirmation that He is faithful! Carmen's words will help lead you down a path to healing where the darkness will fade, and you will experience His Light shining on you once again. With every "Hope-filled Declaration" you make, you will undoubtedly feel your Savior's arms around you as your hurting heart begins to mend.

April Rodgers
Founder of Reflecting Light Ministries

Whether we are growing in our faith or daringly intimate with God, we all encounter those times when we are scorched by a verbal grenade or singed in the fire of despair, defeat, doubts and dead ends. I strongly encourage you to reach for the cooling relief of Carmen's book, *Out of Words*. She describes what we feel and puts our hand into God's. Her prayers are like a fresh rain after a drought that provides a drenching in healing hope. We are soaked in His Presence where she reveals His spoken promises. I plan to give these books to everyone I mentor, lead and love!

Betsy Ringer, Speaker, Author, Personality Specialist, San Diego, CA

This book is like a cold drink of water on a hot day. As I minister to grieving people, I have often looked for books that would comfort their broken hearts without overwhelming their minds. This will definitely be one that I will use often. The constant reference to scripture is so beautiful and comforting! Thank you, Carmen, you are definitely a gift to the broken.

Chaplain Carla Pilgreen

Out of Words: 31 Prayers of Hope for Your Hurting Heart offers the honest, true, and vulnerable prayers you might say during life's most difficult moments when your heart aches and your mind is at a loss for words. While the source of our pain may vary as vast as the sand on the seashore, the answer to all our pain is as consistent as each morning's sunrise and rests in the truths of the creator of both the shore and the sunrise. In each opening vignette, you can tell Carmen has "been there." She knows pain, and she understands. But more importantly, she knows the healer of all our hurts and consistently invites the reader into dialogue, reflection and application of biblical truths with the God of all hope.

Dr. Michelle Bengtson
Board Certified Clinical Neuropsychologist and
author of the award-winning *Hope Prevails: Insights From a Doctor's Personal Journey Through Depression* and *Breaking Anxiety's Grip: How to Reclaim the Peace God Promises.*

When deep heartache and disappointment knocks you on your feet and steals your breath, you likely find yourself speechless, even in prayer. In *Out of Words*, Carmen gives you the actual words to say to help you rediscover prayer in the Prayer Invitation section, as well as comforting your heart with encouraging devotions and offering coaching questions to help you begin to heal your tender heart. Filled with Scripture and Hope-filled Declarations, Out of Words is a must-read for anyone who has ever dealt with a broken heart, disappointment, or grief.

Stephanie K Adams, Real Women Ministries
Author of *In the Shadow of the Cross: Following Jesus Through His Last Days*

Loss. Grief. Anxiety. Confusion. We all experience seasons when painful emotions wrap themselves around our hearts. In *Out of Words*, Carmen invites us to unburden our weary souls and rest in the goodness of God. Written with refreshing honesty, each devotional applies Scriptural truth into wounded places, offering us the fresh hope we desperately crave.

Angela Donadio
Speaker and Author of *Finding Joy When Life is Out of Focus: A Study of Philippians for Joy-Thirsty Women* and *Fearless: Ordinary Women of the Bible who Dared to do Extraordinary Things.*

In her book, Out of Words, Carmen writes "A decision lies before me. Will I gather up all the pieces of my brokenness and lock them tightly within me or will I lay the rubble before You, my good, good Father. Will I trust You to mend what seems unmendable?"

As a mom grieving the loss of my son, I read this and wondered how Carmen knew my heart so well. You will read each tender prayer in amazement. You will want to find Carmen and thank her for guiding you past hurt into the arms of your good Father, where healing is found.

Jodie Barrett
Author of *Jingle and Joy: Praying Beneath the Tree*

Each of us has faced a time (or times) in our life when the hurt we experienced was so deep; we couldn't even put it into words. Carmen meets us in that place – in the midst of the pain – and offers hope. Out of Words provides a daily dose of encouragement for the toughest circumstances. Her easy-to-read format makes it super simple to continue reflecting on each message throughout the day – a must for the busy woman! Through her stories, verses, and points to ponder, I ended each day's reading feeling refreshed and inspired. I plan to read Out of Words again, and again, and again.

Kristine Brown
Pastor's wife, Connect Church Longview, founder of More Than Yourself, Inc. and author of *Over It: Conquering Comparison to Live Out God's Plan*

Out of Words walks step by step through the emotions, questions and struggles of a shattered heart and then serves us Biblical hope straight out of scripture. This life dishes out so much that can break our hearts but we don't have to stay there. In Out of Words, Carmen Horne starts us on a daily practive to take what the enemy would use for harm, offer it to God, and then watch Him turn it around for our good.

Lisa Appelo, speaker and writer

This book is dedicated to the women who have comforted me in my brokenness and to those who have honored me with their trust by inviting me to walk alongside them through their pain.

Friends, you have changed my life.

Dear Jesus,

Anoint these words for Your glory. When my words are inadequate, let the beautiful souls who read them see with eyes of grace. May the very breath of the Holy Spirit whisper healing, comfort, and peace into every person who picks up this book.

I ask this in Your mighty name! Amen.

Table of Contents

A Note From Me

Do you have memories of your first broken heart? Perhaps time has softened some of the sharp edges of your pain, but the memories of my first broken heart remain vivid. In fact, they became more vivid as I matured. I say became, because on the day my heart shattered like a dropped water glass, my little nine-year-old brain did not, simply could not, grasp the depth of hurt and pain that would follow. I can still see my dad sitting on our sofa and hear him saying, "I won't get to see y'all very often." To which I naively replied, "You can pick us up for a visit anytime."

Gradually, I began to realize how a broken home looked and felt. My dad struggled to consistently spend time with us and care for us just as he had struggled with his commitment to his marriage.

My heart has been broken many times since that day. Each time feels like the worst time, until the next time. As the old saying goes, "That which does not kill us, makes us stronger."[i] Believe it or not, this is biblically sound advice.

"Dear brothers and sisters, when troubles of any kind come your way, consider it an opportunity for great joy. For you know that when your faith is tested, your endurance has a chance to grow." (James 1:2-3)

Unfortunately, knowing I'm growing doesn't make the hurt I feel less painful.

Reliving these memories makes my heart deeply tender for you. Because I have been where you are, most of us don't search out a resource for the brokenhearted until the unexpected leaves us breathless. I'm so sorry this life has wounded you.

Our wounds come in many forms. The loss of a breast to cancer can be as devastating as the loss of a marriage to betrayal. My uncle lost his toe to cancer and he spoke often of how much he missed that tiny appendage. A friend lost her job (and her hopes of retiring at a reasonable age) when the company downsized and eliminated her position. In my relationship with my dad, I

1

grieved the loss of what could have been even more than I grieved the loss of his life.

I have faced financial ruin. In our marriage, unaddressed issues grew and my husband and I came so close to divorce, as my momma would say, "It would scare it to death." Illness, betrayal, and a whole host of big and not-so-big hurts have pierced my heart. You and I share membership in the Heartbreak Club. It's neither an exclusive group nor limited in number.

Though more numerous than wildflowers in a field, each and every one of its members has a uniquely painful broken heart story. We can never fully understand other's pain. We must be careful to never minimize their grief. King Solomon reminds us in Proverbs 14:10a, "Each heart knows its own bitterness..."

While we can't share anyone else's specific brand of brokenness what we all have in common is the assurance that our Abba Father understands our individual grief. He has experienced every loss we suffer. Scripture paints a clear picture of how deeply Jesus grieved His followers' heartbreaks, when after speaking with Mary and Martha about the death of their brother, Lazarus, "Jesus wept." (John 11:35)

I'm convinced the prayers God understands most clearly are the tears streaming down our cheeks. Our tears speak volumes, my friend. They are so precious to Him that He collects every one.

"You keep track of all my sorrows. You have collected all my tears in your bottle. You have recorded each one in your book." (Psalm 56:8)

The difficulties we face in finding words to express our pain, even in prayer, or perhaps especially in prayer, can overwhelm most of us. I get that. My pain has rendered me speechless, too. I know what it feels like to be out of words.

Now that my words have returned, in the following pages, I offer you heartfelt encouragement and powerful prayers to help you begin voicing your pain. I simply numbered the segments of this book because I have no expectation that, in your grief, you would have the margin for daily study. You cannot get behind because I only urge you to read them as the Spirit prompts you. When we are sad, the last thing we need is another schedule to keep or list to manage. I know as well as you, falling behind only adds guilt to the heartache and I don't want that for you.

Each segment has a short devotion, prayer, journaling page, and a coaching page with questions to help you process the day and guide your tender heart toward healing. You can use your journal page to write your own prayer or for sorting out your thoughts. I conclude each segment with a Scripture affirmation and a simple hope-filled declaration over your life.

By faith, I believe and declare you will live healed and whole as you relinquish your hurt to the Great Recycler of our pain.

With love, Carmen

If I only touch his garment, I will be made well.

~ Woman with the issue of blood

Matthew 9:21 ESV

One – On Shaky Ground

The Lord is close to the brokenhearted; he rescues those whose spirits are crushed. Psalm 34:18

Have you ever fallen, landed hard, and found it difficult to catch your breath? You "got the wind knocked out of you." That's a perfect description of how it feels when trauma blindsides us.

We feel shaken. The foundation of trust in others, ourselves, or maybe even God, feels compromised. The path ahead looms like a suspended footbridge — shaky and narrow. Each step seems unsupported. We hold on for dear life.

Will we fall like Humpty Dumpty to never be put back together again?

Our dear Father is the Master Repairer of brokenness. He sent Jesus to save those crushed in spirit. Our heart will never be broken beyond God's ability to repair it.

This skill-set is a part of His DNA and godly job description. (Luke 4:18)

These are the times we chose to trust what we know of the character of God instead of our feelings:

- God is Faithful when others are unfaithful.
- God is Love when others are unloving.
- God is Truth when others are dishonest.
- God is Peace when others cause chaos.

Choosing to allow God to begin placing the pieces of our lives back together again begins our healing.

Remember, it is a process. One that takes time. Words may fail you now, but I declare on the basis of God's Word that He will bring rejoicing to your heart again. He will put a new song on your lips as He plants your feet firmly in a foundation of faith.

Prayer Invitation

Heavenly Father,
I am stunned — blindsided. How did this happen? As David said in the Psalms
(22:14), "...my heart is like wax; it is melted within my breast...." Words fail me.
Each time my lips attempt to pray, my brokenness silences them. My heart
pounds and I am breathless with despair. Trembling, tears pour from my eyes.

A decision lies before me. Will I gather up all the pieces of my brokenness and
lock them tightly within me or will I lay the rubble before You, my good, good
Father? Will I trust You to mend what seems un-mendable?

As I lay face down before You Lord, all I can say is, Jesus, help!

In the mighty name of Jesus. Amen.

Pray and Ponder

When Your Words Return:

What does knowing God listens as you pray mean to you? How might this knowledge change the way you pray?

_____

_____

_____

_____

_____

_____

Today I am grateful for:

_____

_____

_____

_____

_____

_____

Scripture Affirmation:

I am my Father's daughter. He always listens to me when I pray. His ear is bent toward my heart. (Psalm 17:6)

Hope-filled Declaration:

You have God's attention. He hangs on your every word.

Two – God Can Handle Our Sadness

If we are unfaithful, he remains faithful, for he cannot deny who he is.
2 Timothy 2:13

Sadness often repels rather than attracts. Friends and family want to find a fix for the brokenness they see in us, but after a period of time, our sadness makes them uncomfortable. Repeatedly searching and failing to find the words to explain a difficult situation begins to feel awkward. There are no words to justify the unjustifiable.

Most of us don't do emotions well. If we can't fix it, we want to walk away from it. Oh, that we could learn the art of a quiet presence.

There is someone who can always handle our sadness. God does not flinch at the sight of our tears. He continues to reach out to us when we try to hide. He not only brings peace, He is Peace — Jehovah Shalom.

God's love is assured. Our questions don't scare Him. He can endure our deafening silences. The wrongs people commit against us makes our heavenly Father angry, too. No one sins against us without also sinning against the Father.

Remember when Jesus overturned the moneychangers' tables in the Temple and drove them, along with the merchants, out with whips? Jesus takes the abuse of His Temple very seriously. (John 2:13-16) After Jesus' crucifixion and resurrection, our hearts became His holy Temple. So, you can imagine how He reacts to the hurts we feel there and the lengths to which He would go to keep our hearts holy and whole.

God is gracious and filled with mercy. Even in our own unfaithfulness to Him, He remains faithful to His promises. He will not leave. Jesus is our real friend who sticks closer than a brother. (Proverbs 18:24)

Prayer Invitation

My God, my God,

Sleep alludes me. My appetite is gone. "My tears have been my food day and night." (Psalm 42:3) As I attempt to wrap my mind around the craziness engulfing me, I hear a still, small voice. Your Holy Spirit reminds me, "I'll never let you down, never walk off and leave you." (Hebrews 13:5 MSG)

Clinging to You, Lord is my only hope.

In the mighty name of Jesus. Amen.

Pray and ponder

When your Words Return:

What question do you have for God? Is there a Bible verse that addresses your question?

Today I am grateful for:

Scripture Affirmation:

God comforts me in my mourning. (Matthew 5:4)

Hope-filled Declaration:

Nothing separates you from God's love.

Three – Grief is Her Name

You know what I long for Lord; you hear my every sigh. Psalm 38:9

Grief attaches herself to every loss. I speak of her as a person because Grief seems to take on a life of her own. She wraps herself around us at every gathering. Grief descends as a heaviness when we try to rest. Our throats close to food when she pulls up a chair beside us at meal time.

We have met her before. Yet, each time we reunite, Grief surprises us with her ability to bring such sorrow.

We grapple with the questions. Why is she allowed entrance into our lives? How can this calamity be used for good? Where was God when Grief ambushed us? Like looking for a missing piece in a puzzle, locating goodness in this badness eludes us. Goodness has been misplaced. If I am honest, God's ways confound me.

When baffled by brokenness, we must look at life through the lens of eternity. We must make a conscious decision to choose the binoculars of faith because the telephoto lens of fear only overwhelms us with hopelessness. (2 Corinthians 4:18)

Thankfully, Grief will not be our constant companion. She may be loud and relentless, but she will not have the last word, friend. Gradually, Grief will become quieter and feel more distant.

In Psalm 30:5, David sings, "Weeping may last for the night, but joy comes in the morning." Morning may not be tomorrow for you, but there will be a day when darkness drifts away and joy rises like the sun in the Eastern sky.

Prayer Invitation

Loving Shepherd,

Sadness closes up my throat. I try to swallow and tears threaten to prevent it. Grief ambushes me. Like a thief, she sneaks up and pounces when I least expect it. She descends with heaviness.

Yet, through the blanket of heaviness, I feel Your presence, Lord. As I walk through this dark valley, I remind myself You are with me. As my Shepherd, Your protection is not only for my physical body but for the restoration of my soul. (Psalm 23) Each day You carry me in Your arms. (Psalm 68:19b)

I praise You even in my sadness.

In the mighty name of Jesus. Amen.

Pray and ponder

When your Words Return:

What is one way you are working through your grief?

_____

_____

_____

_____

_____

_____

Today, I am grateful for:

_____

_____

_____

_____

_____

Scripture Affirmation:

God cares about my troubles and He cares about the anguish of my soul.
(Psalm 31:7)

Hope-filled Declaration:

Nothing escapes God's loving eyes. You are His focus.

Four – Peace Despite Chaos

Now may the Lord of peace himself give you peace at all times in every way.
The Lord be with you all. 2 Thessalonians 3:16 ESV

How do we find calm in chaos? The saying goes, "Not my circus, not my monkeys."ⁱⁱ Well, what if it is our circus? What if we have found ourselves smack dab in the middle of our very own carnival sideshow?

The thing is, nothing happening under this big top feels like fun and games. We are like tightrope walkers with frayed ropes.

The Apostle Paul often found himself in tumultuous times. On house arrest and in chains for Christ he wrote the letter to the church at Philippi. In this setting he penned,

Don't worry about anything; instead, pray about everything. Tell God what you need, and thank him for all he has done. Then you will experience God's peace, which exceeds anything we can understand. His peace will guard your hearts and minds as you live in Christ Jesus. (Philippians 4:6-7)

I wish I could explain the peace of God, but Scripture tells us it passes all understanding. What I do know is that I have experienced peace when my life and circumstances were in total disarray. Lying on my tear-soaked pillow, I chose to shift my gaze from my sorrow and fix my eyes on Jesus. (Hebrews 12:2)

Call out to Him when you are frazzled. He does not suggest; He commands us to cast our anxieties on Him. (1 Peter 5:7) He can untangle the tangled. He can help us change our perspective on the unexpected. He can turn our circus into a sermon.

Our heavenly Father knows the answers when we can't even comprehend the questions. As my dear friend, Sister Odeal, always said, "He will do to depend on."

Prayer Invitation

Dear Lord,

I feel like my rope is frayed and I am hanging on by a thread. Will You hold me tight? Will You help me feel Your presence when all the other feels of life are weighing me down? I claim David's declaration in Psalm 6:9 as my own, "The Lord has heard my plea; the Lord will answer my prayer."

You have never failed me. I am depending on You, now.

In the mighty name of Jesus. Amen.

Pray and ponder

When your Words Return:

What is one worry you can release to God today?

Today, I am grateful for:

Scripture Affirmation:

God takes my burdens and in return gives me rest. (Matthew 11:28)

Hope-filled Declaration:

You belong to a gentle Heavenly Father.

Five – Calming an Anxious Mind

For God gave us a spirit not of fear but of power and love and self-control.
2 Timothy 1:7 ESV

The cool wall tile felt good against my cheek. Tears poured silently. *Don't wake the family.* I did not want them to ask questions requiring answers.

When anxiety and fear bang against our hearts like an unlatched screen door caught by the wind, we start looking for something to secure it. Jesus, my friend, is our latch. He calms the wind. Jesus guards the door of our hearts.

What are some ways Jesus secures our peace? If we look to Scripture, David often used music. He was a prolific songwriter and the Psalms were his songbook.

A beloved children's hymn has quieted my anguish many times. Sometimes sung silently, but with deep thankfulness for the truth in its comforting chorus.

> "Jesus loves me, this I know,
> for the Bible tells me so.
> Little ones to him belong;
> they are weak, but he is strong.
> Refrain:
> Yes, Jesus loves me! Yes, Jesus loves me!
> Yes, Jesus loves me! The Bible tells me so."[iii]

Over and over these simple words fill my mind with truth and block out the voice of my enemy. It's amazing how we can capture thoughts and calm an overactive mind with a sweet, little Jesus song.

Let me encourage you to think of ways to take your thoughts captive. Music, memorizing Scripture, or activities that require us to think (crafts, puzzles, etc.) are good for calming our racing minds. With intention, we can control our thoughts.

Prayer Invitation

Dear Abba Father,

I am too distressed to pray. I'm scared, anxious, and I long for Your comfort. Thoughts, images, and circumstances play on repeat in my mind. Anxiety is robbing me of logic.

I must take these thoughts captive. Help me believe the truth of the children's song "Jesus Loves Me This I Know."

Hug me tight, Lord. I need to feel Your love so I will not be overcome with hopelessness.

I will write God's "faithful love endures forever" on the sticky notes of my heart. (Psalm 117:2)

In the mighty name of Jesus. Amen.

Pray and ponder

When Your Words Return:

Name one thing you can do today to capture your anxious thoughts.

_____

_____

_____

_____

_____

Today, I am grateful for:

_____

_____

_____

_____

Scripture Affirmation:

The Holy Spirit equips me with tools to grab my unhealthy thoughts and
replace them with healthy ones.
(2 Corinthians 10:5)

Hope-filled Declaration:

You have the fruit of self-control. Your thoughts are healthy.

I am a woman
troubled in spirit...
I have been pouring
out my soul
before the Lord.

~ Hannah

1 Samuel 1:15 ESV

Six – Running from Pain

For I am the Lord who heals you. Exodus 15:26

One of the temptations in emotional pain is to look for the nearest and easiest painkiller. Who welcomes suffering?

My friend, who is a recovering addict, shared this truth from his life, "I drank and took drugs to keep the blinds pulled on my life. When I started getting sober, the blinds lifted and the light came in."

Some of the things we use to run from our pain are alcohol, drugs (prescription or illegal), relationships, excess shopping, overeating, power...Anything that keeps us from having to feel.

The Samaritan woman (John 4:4-26) tried to fill her emptiness with unhealthy relationships. Saul fought his fear with abuse of power. (1 Samuel 18:29) Despite God's promise of a child, Sarai's (Sarah) pain over infertility made the idea of using a surrogate (Hagar) appealing. (Genesis 16)

Dr. Chris Thurman believes emotional pain can be helpful.[iv] It sounds an alarm to alert us there is something we need to tend. Running from emotional issues and bypassing healthy healing processes only leaves us with deeper wounds.

Two helpful thoughts as we face painful issues:
- Just as with a physical wound, our emotional wounds need tending. They fester when ignored.
- Well-tended wounds minimize scarring.

Run to God instead of running from pain. With Him, we can face anything because He gives us the strength we need to stop running and process the hurt. (Philippians 4:13)

Prayer Invitation

Dear God,

There is a deep emptiness in my heart and I wonder how it will be filled. The enemy of my soul has an arsenal of soothing elixirs to ease my pain. I declare, "Get behind me, Satan. I do not belong to you, I belong to God!" (Matthew 4:10)

Empower me, Holy Spirit, to only seek comfort from godly sources. Remind me, day and night, true peace and healing will only come from and through my relationship with You. (Romans 8:6)

In the mighty name of Jesus. Amen.

Pray and ponder

When Your Words Return:

Are you filling an emptiness or running from your pain in an unhealthy way? If so, what one thing can you do to change your behavior?

_____

_____

_____

_____

_____

_____

Today, I am grateful for:

_____

_____

_____

_____

_____

Scripture Affirmation:

My relationship with Jesus fills any empty place within my soul. He is the bread of life and living water. (John 6:35; 4:14)

Hope-filled Declaration:

God fills your cup to overflowing with blessings.

Seven – Feeling Numb

But you, O Lord, are a shield about me,
my glory, and the lifter of my head. Psalm 3:3 ESV

Emotional numbness naturally occurs after trauma. Some call it shock. Seth J. Gillihan, Ph.D. explains, "Part of the numbing response can come from the body and mind's self-protective efforts in the face of overwhelming emotions."[v]

When hurt settles in like the oppressive heat of a summer day, our emotions vary widely and change without warning. We can go from numb to heartbroken to happy in the span of a few minutes. We must resist the urge to place them on a neat little schedule we can check off our to-do list.

Instead, let's learn to feel how we feel. If that's numb, know that numb is a feeling and it's perfectly normal. A routine blood test once left the palm of my hand numb. The needle angered the nerve. I discovered that numb was a stage of healing.

We may never understand why we must walk this broken road. As we approach the fork in any painful path, the best choice is always the way of trust. Think back on God's past faithfulness. Trust Him to do it again.

Having an honest conversation with our heavenly Father keeps the doors of communication open. Confiding in Him as we would our dear friend allows the Holy Spirit an opportunity to give direction and comfort. Jesus introduced Him as our Comforter. Let's allow Him to do His job in our lives by turning to Him with trust during times of trouble.

God created us to feel deeply. He also designed our minds to experience periods of numbness after trauma to protect themselves until we can process our feelings. He understands we need His gentle care to navigate the many nuances of our emotions.

Prayer Invitation

Heavenly Father,

I am so sad. Yet often I feel numb. Where are You, Lord? Your Word says You direct my steps. (Psalm 37:23) Why must I walk this path? I don't understand.

As my mind whirls, I choose to trust You, Lord. Our relationship is not based on feelings. It is based on truth. I know You are faithful, loving, and trustworthy. When I am filled with doubt, hold me tighter, please. (Mark 9:24)

You, Lord, are my strength and shield. I adore You.

In the mighty name of Jesus. Amen.

Pray and Ponder

When your words return:

What feelings and emotions are you ignoring? Invite God into a conversation about ways to process them.

_____

_____

_____

_____

_____

_____

Today, I am grateful for:

_____

_____

_____

_____

_____

Scripture Affirmation:

Jesus promised I will one day see clearly what I see dimly now. I trust Him to be
the light on my path forward.
(1 Corinthians 13:12; Psalm 119:105)

Hope-filled Declaration:

Your emotions are a gift from God.

Eight - Irreplaceable Loss

The thief comes only to steal and kill and destroy. I came that they may have life and have it abundantly. John 10:10 ESV

Sometimes this life steals from us what it can never replace. If someone took money or an item that did not belong to them, restitution is possible. But how do we handle the feelings that flood in when what's been stolen cannot be replaced? Grieving parents, abused children, and betrayed spouses know first-hand the crushing sadness of irreplaceable loss.

Speaking from experience, no immediate answer will take away the heartbreak or the questions that follow. Just as Paul exhorts the church at Philippi (2:12) to work out their salvation with fear and trembling, I believe we work out our healing through tears and many conversations with God.

A good place to begin is an understanding that Satan is the one ultimately responsible for our irreplaceable losses. He uses those who will allow him access, but he is the master thief. Our misfortune is not God's will.

He created us with a good plan for our lives. A future filled with hope. (Jeremiah 29:11) He is as outraged with evil as we are. In Matthew 18:6, Jesus is blunt — harm My children and drowning would be a better outcome. His chastisement of the Jewish leaders who mistreated God's people and His defense of the adulterous woman spoke volumes about His regard for equal justice. (John 8:1-11)

Ultimately, we choose, by faith, to believe God will right every wrong. (1 Peter 4:5)

Resentment over an irreplaceable loss is normal. Normal, but harmful to our health. If we allow those feelings to linger too long, we can do physical and emotional harm to ourselves. Leaving justice to God allows us time to focus on healing.

Releasing our empty heart and hands to Jesus will be an act of obedience and sacrifice. Take it one day at a time. He understands each of us process emotions differently.

Prayer Invitation

Dear Lord,

My heart is broken and yet the world goes on. I look around me and think, "Do you people realize that I will never be the same? That what I have lost can never be returned?"

How will I go forward after such a loss? Who will repay what the enemy of my soul has stolen from me? I will stand on this promise, Lord, "God, your God, will restore everything you lost; he'll have compassion on you; he'll come back and pick up the pieces from all the places where you were scattered." (Deuteronomy 30:3 MSG)

I'm so thankful for this promise in Your Word, Lord, because I sure feel scattered.

In the mighty name of Jesus. Amen.

Pray and ponder

When your words return:

What one thing can you do to release to God the bitter feelings over your irreplaceable loss?

Today, I am grateful for:

Scripture Affirmation:

God is kind and supportive. My foundation is firm. I am being restored and strengthened. (1 Peter 5:10)

Hope-filled Declaration:

God will restore every broken place within you.

Nine - Rusty Weapons

For the weapons of our warfare are not of the flesh but
have divine power to destroy strongholds.
2 Corinthians 10:4 ESV

In difficult times we hope our faith will rise to defend us from attack. During a painful time in my life, I realized my spiritual weapons had become weakened by lack of use. When life was easy, I neglected the spiritual disciplines that kept me fit for battle. It was as if I'd left my weapons out in the rain to rust.

So, how do we rise for battle when the enemy crests our hill of complacency?

- The best time to sharpen our weapons is before we are thrust into battle. Bible reading and prayer today helps us be ready tomorrow.
- Who we often think is our enemy, is not our real enemy. Satan prowls around looking for someone to devour. (1 Peter 5:8) He is the enemy.
- Even in the midst of the attack, it's not too late to sharpen our weapons. Pain is a grand motivator.

Putting our dukes up will not defeat the enemy. The devil fights dirty. He uses hurt, pain, disappointment, and discouragement to cripple his opponent. He works to oppress us and silence our testimony — a defeated foe attempting to undermine what God is doing in our lives.

But, our victory is secure. The One who lives in us is greater than the one that lives in this world. (1 John 4:4)

The Holy Spirit empowers us to resist the devil. Jesus resisted by using Scripture. When we use the Word as our offensive weapon, the Holy Spirit empowers our choices. No weapon forged against us will succeed. (Isaiah 54:17)

The enemy keeps his weapons sharp. To defeat him we must rid our weapons of the rust of complacency and be prepared to fight with the whole armor of God. (Ephesians 6:13-18)

Prayer Invitation

Mighty God,

Spiritually I feel weak, Lord. I am in a battle I didn't choose and I feel like I am fighting with rusty weapons. I need Your help to gather my arsenal. Help me to remember that Satan is my true enemy. Don't let me fix my eyes on the one who hurt me, but instead, fix my eyes on You, the author and perfecter of my faith. (Hebrews 12:2)

Every piece of Your armor, Lord, will help me resist this spiritual attack. (Ephesians 6:11) After this battle, Lord, I want to be found standing firm. (Ephesians 6:13)

In the mighty name of Jesus. Amen.

Pray and ponder

When your words return:

List each piece of God's armor made available to you and consider ways you could use them in the battle you face today. (Ephesians 6:10-18)

_____

_____

_____

_____

_____

_____

Today, I am grateful for:

_____

_____

_____

_____

_____

Scripture Affirmation:

The Lord is my strength and protection. He helps me and fills my heart with joy.
(Psalms 28:7)

Hope-filled Declaration:

God equips you to win any spiritual battle.

Ten – So Long Anxiety

The name of the Lord is a strong tower; the righteous man runs into it and is safe. Proverbs 18:10 ESV

Hard times can birth the belief that we live under Murphy's law[vi] instead of God's providence. The dread of waiting on the next shoe to drop keeps us on high alert. *"What next?"*, we ask ourselves.

In the book *Anxious for Nothing*[vii], we read, "Anxiety and fear are cousins but not twins. Fear sees a threat. Anxiety imagines one. Fear screams, *Get Out!* Anxiety ponders, *What if?*"

Anxiety saps our strength.[viii] It makes us weary. To me, there is a difference between tired and weary. Weary is soul tired. The kind of tired not even eight straight hours of sleep can cure.

When I was a little girl, I slept with my Gideon Bible[ix] under my pillow. Like a favorite blanket or doll, having it near me made me feel safe. I was on the right track to finding security — a relationship with Jesus.

As I've become a more mature woman, I've discovered releasing our anxieties to our Abba Father requires intentionality. Learning to recognize our security is in Christ alone is a hard-won battle. One we often go toe-to-toe with day after day.

Instead of asking ourselves "what if" and "what's next" we ought to be asking ourselves these two questions.

1) What is the truth in our situation?
2) How likely is it that what we fear will happen?

No terrifying scenario we can conjure up changes the truth of who God is or His love for us. We rarely realize our worst fears, though they torment us relentlessly. Honestly answering these two questions helps us say so long to anxiety.

Prayer Invitation

My Lord,

Lord, thank You for comforting me when fear overwhelms my heart. Anxiety over what's next has my insides trembling. The old hymn says I can come to You "Just as I Am."ˣ I'm too exhausted to pretend, "just as I am" for me right now is weary.

Thank You for meeting me here. My weakness is an opportunity for Your strength to be made real in me. (2 Corinthians 12:9)

In the mighty name of Jesus. Amen.

Pray and ponder

When your words return:

Write Isaiah 26:3 below. Describe how keeping your thoughts fixed on Jesus might help you say so long to anxiety.

_____

_____

_____

_____

_____

_____

Today, I am grateful for:

_____

_____

_____

_____

_____

Scripture Affirmation:

I am not afraid or discouraged because I belong to Jesus. He strengthens me and holds me with His strong right hand. (Isaiah 41:10)

Hope-filled Declaration:

God renews your strength.

In the silence
of the heart,
God speaks.

~ Mother Teresa

Eleven – Feeling Alone

Nevertheless, I am continually with you; you hold my right hand.
Psalm 73:23 ESV

Loneliness often accompanies loss. We can be surrounded by people and still feel alone. Where does that feeling come from?

Loss leaves a void that surrounds our souls with a denseness, like a fog gathering after a morning rain. Once loneliness hovers over our hearts, it is hard to see past it and we often miss the sweet blessings around us.

When wounded, withdrawing seems logical. Then, Satan uses our loneliness against us to discourage us even further. From there, it doesn't take long before we lose hope. Hopelessness often brings an even greater desire for seclusion, and the cycle spirals out of control. If our loss involves abandonment, in an attempt for self-preservation, we might think, *"who needs people, anyway?"*

We need people, that is who. We are better and stronger together. (Ecclesiastes 4:9)

Although we may be lonely at times, we are never truly alone — Jehovah Shammah — God is there.

Caregiving for my mom solidified this belief within me.

In the aloneness of the valley of the shadow of death, my momma felt God's presence. I was always near, but in truth, the journey from this world to the next is a walk we travel with our Savior alone. She testified to feeling Him next to her as she slept. She said, "I try not to move because I don't want to disturb Him. I want Him to stay." God brought her comfort and in turn, He brought me comfort.

"Snuggle in God's arms. When you are hurting, when you feel lonely, left out. Let him cradle you, comfort you, reassure you of His all sufficient power and love."[xi]

Prayer Invitation

Jehovah Shammah,

I feel so lonely. Even when I'm around others, I feel alone. My friends invite me for a visit. My family stops by to see how I am. Lonesomeness sits heavy on my chest. The indentation of the missing piece in my life seems cavernous. I'm feeling discouraged. Please fill this emptiness in me with Your love. (Romans 5:5)

Lord, You have promised to always be near. (Matthew 28:20) I know You are there because I stand on your promise to never leave.

In the mighty name of Jesus. Amen.

Pray and Ponder

When your words return:

To whom can you reach out to ease your loneliness? Who might need you to reach out to and ease their loneliness?

_____

_____

_____

_____

_____

_____

Today, I am grateful for:

_____

_____

_____

_____

_____

Scripture Affirmation:

When I walk through dark valleys, I am not alone. God is with me. (Psalm 23:4)

Hope-filled Declaration:

God's presence replaces your loneliness.

Twelve – The Mystery of God's Provision

Oh, how great are God's riches and wisdom and knowledge! How impossible it is for us to understand his decisions and his ways! Romans 11:33

Naaman's healing came from the mud of the Jordan River. Ruth's restoration was ushered in by Boaz, a relative of her mother-in-law, Naomi. Jochebed's son, Moses', life was saved by the very people who ordered his death. In my life, the events I thought would destroy our family, brought instead a greater awareness of the hard and sacred gift of commitment.

We dishonor God's sovereignty when we assign coincidence or luck to our life. God promises that He directs the steps of the godly and delights in every detail of our lives. (Psalm 37:23) When we acknowledge Him working specifically for us, it makes it easier to have eyes that see His handiwork.

God's provisions are not coincidences.

We can't assume God's provisions will arrive in any certain way. He sends what we need, when we need it, in the way He knows will benefit us the most. The thing is, in our everyday walking around life, God's care looks a lot like our friends and family. Jesus told us to love one another. To me, that translates into not only caring for others but allowing others to care for us.

Each time we receive a call, text, card, hug, or visit from someone who cares for us, it is actually a loving touch from our heavenly Father. He uses those who are willing to be his hands and feet. Take time to recognize God's intentional provision through those who love you.

A wonderful prayer for us to regularly pray is, *Lord, open my eyes to Your work in my life.*

Prayer Invitation

Abba Father,

I need the comfort of my Daddy God. A comfort only You can give. I accept it in whatever form You send — a prayer, a hug, a card, a text, or a call. Don't let me dismiss as coincidence Your touch. (Proverbs 19:21) Lord, I don't want to miss Your handiwork because it comes in different packaging than I expect.

You care for the birds and flowers and You will care for me. (Matthew 10:29-31) I am depending on You. I believe You will provide everything I need.

In the mighty name of Jesus. Amen.

Pray and ponder

When your words return:

Can you name one way God has used others to express His love for you?

_____

_____

_____

_____

_____

_____

_____

Today, I am grateful for:

_____

_____

_____

_____

_____

Scripture Affirmation:

I share the burdens of others and I allow others to share mine. (Galatians 6:2)

Hope-filled Declaration:

God places people in your life to show you His love.

Thirteen – Burdens too Heavy to Carry

Come with me by yourselves to a quiet place and get some rest.
Matthew 6:31 NIV

When Christians speak of adversity, they often misquote 1 Corinthians 10:13 by saying, "God won't give you more than you can handle." Well, I don't know about you, but I have felt like the bottom man in a football pile-up. The heaviness left me unable to move.

The Apostle Paul, in 2 Corinthians 1:8-9, was given more than he could handle, "We were crushed and overwhelmed beyond our ability to endure, and we thought we would never live through it. In fact, we expected to die." Thank you, Paul, for your transparency or we might think our feelings of despair are uncommon.

As Paul continues to share his story, he tells us how he survived and how we can too:

- Rely on God and not on ourselves.
- Remember God's track record. He has rescued us in the past and He will rescue us again.
- Request prayer. Take comfort in the fact that others can help by praying for us.
- Rejoice in hope. The answers we receive will encourage others.

Paul testified to his feelings of despair, and the valuable lesson he learned about how to rely on God instead of himself. Life in this world will give us more than we can handle, by ourselves. Our endurance depends, not on ourselves, but rather on our unwavering belief in the omnipotence, omniscience, and omnipresence of God.

God lightens our burdens by strengthening our faith in His supreme wisdom, power, and presence.

Prayer Invitation

Dear Lord,

The load I'm carrying is more than I can bear and I'm near despair, Lord. You promise Your yoke is easy and Your burden is light. (Matthew 11:30) Please lift this weight I carry and help me to place it at Your feet. I need You to remind me to breathe. I'm depending on Your promises to see me through these dark days. (2 Corinthians 1:20)

Help me to release my burdens to You and exchange them for soul rest.

In the mighty name of Jesus. Amen.

Pray and Ponder

When your words return:

What does it mean to you to release your burden to God?

_____
_____
_____
_____
_____
_____

Today, I am grateful for:

_____
_____
_____
_____
_____

Scripture Affirmation:

I release my burdens to You, Lord, and in return, I receive Your rest.
(Matthew 11:28)

Hope-filled Declaration:

God makes your heart lighter and your way clearer.

Fourteen – On Asking Why

The Lord works out everything to its proper end. Proverbs 16:4 NIV

Naturally, we want the answer to our most pressing question: why? For most of us, it is our first question. Why didn't the God of the universe protect our little patch of earth during this soul-shaking experience? Why didn't He do something?

We know He can, but why does He not?

I have lain face down on the carpet myself — stunned by the craziness unfolding around me.

Standing in the shower (my cry room) I have declared to God, "If my daughter needed something, I would do everything in my power to provide it. I'm your child, why are you silent?" May I give you a few thoughts I have wrestled out for myself?

We wouldn't understand.

If God shared His reasoning with us, I doubt we would agree. We need God to be God because He is wise beyond our understanding. (Romans 11:13, ESV) Like a Master Baker, He incorporates all the ingredients of our lives, sweet and bitter, and creates a masterpiece that will be used for His glory. (Romans 8:28)

His knowledge is too great for us.

We are ill-equipped to know how this will play out in our future. In His wisdom, God protects us from revelations that would cause despair. If I had known some of the things I have faced, before I faced them, I would have lost all heart to go on.

So much of the Christian walk involves trust. One day, we will understand. (1 Corinthians 13:12) Until then, we choose to believe in God's goodness and love, even when we long to know why we must endure pain and suffering.

Prayer Invitation

Sovereign Lord,

Do You have an answer to my biggest question? Why? Day and night, I search for understanding. These thoughts consume me. I don't get it. Is there an answer? (Psalm 5:1-2)

For my sanity, I choose to trust You, Lord. My confidence in Your love and faithfulness remains even in the face of such uncertainty and confusion. As the three men declared before they were thrown into the fiery furnace, "But, if not..." (Daniel 3:18) I want an answer, "But if not..." my love for You endures.

In the mighty name of Jesus. Amen.

Pray and Ponder

When your words return:

How would knowing the answer to your biggest "why?" change your situation today?

_____
_____
_____
_____
_____
_____

Today, I am grateful for:

_____
_____
_____
_____
_____

Scripture Affirmation:

I serve a great God! His power is absolute! My hope is in God's unfailing love.
(Psalm 147:5;11)

Hope-filled Declaration:

Your trust and honor bring God delight.

Fifteen – Banish Bitterness and Sarcasm

Watch out that no poisonous root of bitterness grows up to trouble you, corrupting many. Hebrews 12:15b

Bitterness and her first cousin, Sarcasm, have deep roots we can trace back to their predecessor, Hurt.

Sarcasm smiles and stings, while Bitterness lashes out. Sarcasm pretends. Bitterness cannot hide her disdain.

Sarcasm is our unpredictable friend. She makes us laugh, even if it's an uncomfortable chuckle. She hides her pain-inflicting agenda by assuring us no offense was meant. "It was all a joke, OK?"

We see Sarcasm as our protector. With her by our side, we feel empowered as she erects walls to protect our hearts.

The ugliness of Bitterness is exhaustive and far-reaching. Her words are meant to hurt. She is unable to forgive offenses and destroys all who allow her residence. Bitterness will not let us forget our pain. The memories of it fuel her.

So, how do we rid ourselves of these two meanies?

Here are three things we can do to start the eviction:

1. Search our hearts and invite God to clean them up. Luke 6:45b says, "What you say flows from what is in your heart."
2. Choose forgiveness. God requires it and we need it for our health. Pray for the ones we can't forgive. God knows. God heals.
3. Think before we speak. Am I trying to hurt? Will these words improve my life or be used to keep me in captivity?

The more we refuse to let Bitterness and Sarcasm rule, the easier to control they will become. Banishing them releases a healing blessing over our lives.

Prayer Invitation

Patient Father,

I realize Bitterness has become my companion. She is demanding and never lets me forget the details of my hurt. What do I do with those memories, Lord?

How do I choose forgiveness? I'm keeping score and that's unhealthy. (1 Corinthians 13:5) Forgive me, Lord! Help me to love when I feel unloving.

Reveal the hidden agenda of Sarcasm in my life. Shine the bright light of Your conviction on my habit of using her methods to sting others instead of handling my emotions in a healthy way. Take control of what I say and guard my speech. (Psalm 141:3)

As I follow Your lead, Bitterness and Sarcasm will be replaced with peace. Thank you for Your patience, Lord.

In the mighty name of Jesus. Amen.

Pray and ponder

When your words return:

How will evicting Bitterness and Sarcasm improve your quality of life?

_____

_____

_____

_____

_____

Today I am grateful for:

_____

_____

_____

_____

Scripture Affirmation:

I trust in the Lord and do good. I turn from my anger. I commit everything to God and He helps me. (Psalm 37:3, 5, 8a)

Hope-filled Declaration:

God transforms your bitterness and sarcasm into joy.

The prayer of a righteous woman has great power as it is working.

James 5:16 ESV
(gender change mine)

Sixteen - Not So Sweet Revenge

Don't say, 'I will get even for this wrong.' Wait for the Lord to handle the matter. Proverbs 20:22

Why does revenge seem so sweet?

We often think if we can hurt them as much as they have hurt us, we will feel better. As I ponder a time of deep emotional pain in my life, gathering a list of hurtful things to say weighed heavy on my mind. I wanted to be mean, you know?

One of the questions we should ask ourselves when our hearts are full of hurt aching to spill from our mouths is, "Will my words change the situation for the better?" I'm not talking about speaking truth to resolve a situation, I'm talking about lashing out to cause pain.

The saying, "A man who desires revenge should dig two graves"[xii] (to borrow from an old-timer's saying), "will preach." Trying to get even eventually weakens the avenger even more. Our Bible assures us that God handles vengeance. He is the ultimate Righter of all wrongs. (Romans 12:19)

Handling conflict in a healthy way involves communication. We should push pause when we realize we are not ready to speak the truth in love. Step away until we can speak using self-control. The tongue is little but mighty. It can change conversation to consternation and communication to conflict. (James 3:1-12)

Realizing revenge is never as sweet as it seems, helps us practice self-control and release our desire for justice to the only One qualified to judge.

Prayer Invitation

Mighty Father,

I'm hurt. Can I turn my hurt over to You? I can't do this on my own. If I am honest, I want revenge! Calm me, dear Jesus. Quiet the waves of anger that overwhelm, please! (Psalm 4:4)

I trust You to handle the messiness of my life and heal my brokenness. You are the expert on forgiving. Empower me to do what seems impossible. (Matthew 19:26) I'm depending on You, Lord.

In the mighty name of Jesus. Amen.

Pray and ponder

When your Words Return:

Are you approaching your desire for justice as an opportunity for revenge or for healthy confrontation?

Today, I am grateful for:

Scripture Affirmation:

I do not seek revenge. My choices reflect honor. (Romans 12:17)

Hope-filled Declaration:

Your self-control is a witness to others.

seventeen - Sleepless nights

But Jesus replied, 'My Father is always working, and so am I.' John 5:17

I like to help God. Don't you?

Often it seems like I have the perfect idea to solve my problem. I just need to clue God in on my solution. My nickname could be "junior god."

Psalm 121 is a mere eight verses, but those eight verses are powerful affirmations of God's provision and protection. "Indeed, he who watches over Israel never slumbers or sleeps." (Psalm 121:4)

When we grasp this beautiful concept, we embrace a welcomed blessing. We can lay our head on our pillow each night and look forward to the opportunity for renewal.

When we forget He is alert, present, and always working, we lose sleep.

God created sleep to equip us for the day ahead, but too often we forfeit it with our anxious thoughts.

Losing sleep diminishes our ability to take on the challenges that come with grief and loss. All our attempts to help God, only hurt ourselves.

Imagine how making the choice to grab hold of God's promises could change the quality of the life we live today. "A peaceful heart leads to a healthy body..." (Proverbs 14:30a)

We need peace. We need to know that when we have no clue, God is working. To believe this we must have faith; we must trust; we must make a choice.

Relax and rest in God's care. He's got this and He doesn't need our help.

Prayer Invitation

Heavenly Father,

I am not sleeping well. My thoughts of the future are robbing me of rest. Each day brings many questions and I feel an overwhelming responsibility to have all the answers. So many times, my heart responds, "I don't know." (Matthew 6:34)

Momma always said, "If you can get a good night's sleep, you can handle most anything." You created sleep to restore me physically and emotionally. Lord, I need to sleep! (Psalm 3:5)

Settle my mind, please. Make my eyes heavy as I praise You for the beautiful gift of rest.

In the mighty name of Jesus. Amen.

Pray and ponder

When your Words Return:

Create a list of Bible verses on rest and peace to read each night before bed. Using at least one of them, create a personalized Scripture prayer.

Today, I am grateful for:

Scripture Affirmation:

When I lie down, I am not afraid. My sleep is sweet.
(Proverbs 3:24)

Hope-filled Declaration:

God takes your burdens and gives you rest.

Eighteen - Stop Rehearsing Hurt

Think about things that are excellent and worthy of praise.
Philippians 4:8b

One of the most helpful actions we can take to reframe our perspective on difficult circumstances is to stop rehearsing them.

Sad, hopeless feelings drift in like dark clouds across the fertile lands of our memories as we replay every brutal detail of the situations that battered and bruised our hearts. We become angry again using the painful script we have memorized. Our hurts become even more vivid during that kind of rehearsal.

Oh, friends, it doesn't have to be this way. We can choose to guard our hearts. Putting 2 Corinthians 10:5 into action we can learn to take our thoughts captive,

We destroy arguments and every lofty opinion raised against the knowledge of God, and take every thought captive to obey Christ, (ESV)

What might that look like in real life?

- Talking to ourselves. "I forgave that. I will not rehearse those hurts." Repeat as many times as necessary.
- Looking for truth. What do we know versus how do we feel?
- Praying – Communicating our struggles to God and asking Him to reveal His truth to us.
- Reading books and seeking counsel from godly men and women

We forfeit rest with anxious thoughts.

Every time we rehearse hurt, we re-open our wounds. And friends, our wounds might be in the beginning stages of healing. We can't always keep others from tearing into our tender places, but we can stop ourselves from re-opening old wounds. We have the power to choose!

Resist the urge to rehearse your hurt by replacing those tired lines with God's truth.

Prayer Invitation

Dear Lord,

I'm mad today. As I think about this mayhem in my life, anger rises within me. Forgiveness that seemed likely yesterday, is far away today as I rehearse my hurt. The script of my pain has been all too easy to memorize, but I want to replace it with Your truth. I cry out to You for help. (Proverbs 4:25-26)

I will not relinquish control of my emotions to others. I choose joy, peace, and love through the power of the Holy Spirit. (Romans 15:13) I am believing for Holy Spirit power to fill me today!

In the mighty name of Jesus. Amen.

Pray and Ponder

When your words return:

Can you name one truth you learned about yourself or God during a difficult time? How can you use that truth to re-write the negative script on replay in your mind?

_____

_____

_____

_____

_____

_____

Today, I am thankful for:

_____

_____

_____

_____

_____

Scripture Affirmation:

My focus is on truth. I think about the lovely things in my life. (Philippians 4:8)

Hope-filled Declaration:

God is writing a beautiful story in your life.

Nineteen – Feeling Abandoned

No, I will not abandon you as orphans – I will come to you. John 14:18

My heart is tender for the men who walked away from so much in their private lives to follow a man who rocked the world everywhere He went. There was so much excitement and intrigue. They had plans and Jesus leaving them was not a part of the strategy.

Jesus knew they would feel abandoned. He understood their feelings of confusion and disappointment over how He handled the situations they faced.

Our circumstances can make us feel deserted too. When we are facing uncertain times, we long to feel God's presence.

What Jesus promised the disciples is what He promises us:

"I'm leaving you well and whole. That's my parting gift to you. Peace. I don't leave you the way you're used to being left— feeling abandoned, bereft. So, don't be upset. Don't be distraught." (John 14:27 MSG)

When Jesus told them this, He understood their expectations. He also knew He could not meet them in the way they thought He would.

In God's wisdom, He may choose to meet our needs in ways we don't recognize at first. Can we open our hearts to the unexpected answers sent our way?

God is always near. Inviting Him to open our spiritual eyes to His presence is an opportunity to change our perspective on His work in our lives. In light of this new perspective, we can exchange our feelings of abandonment for the reality of His constant companionship through the Holy Spirit.

Prayer Invitation

Heavenly Father,

I'm so confused and disappointed. I feel like an orphan — alone and deserted. My expectations of how others would behave have been dashed. If I'm honest, my expectations of how You would respond have been turned upside down. (Luke 7:23)

Since I'm having trouble seeing You in my situation, will You please reveal Yourself to me? I'm asking for confirmation of Your presence. I will not trust my own understanding. I will trust You to direct my path. (Proverbs 3:5-6)

In the mighty name of Jesus. Amen.

Pray and ponder

When your words return:

In your present circumstances, when and how has God used others to be His hands and feet in your life?

_____

_____

_____

_____

_____

Today, I am grateful for:

_____

_____

_____

_____

Scripture Affirmation:

I have a relationship with God. I trust Him to never abandon me. (Psalm 9:10)

Hope-filled Declaration:

God is with you wherever you go.

Twenty – Finding a New Normal

Behold, I am doing a new thing; now it springs forth, do you not perceive it? I will make a way in the wilderness and rivers in the desert. Isaiah 43:19 ESV

"Things will not go back to the way they were. You must make a new normal," he said. And, I was left to wonder what that looked like.

In the most hurt filled times in my life, I wanted normal. I wanted what was, not what it had become.

Change is hard. I wish it was not so uncomfortable. Don't you? We want it to slip on like a pair of well-worn jeans. Instead, it feels like a stiff shirt that never seems to soften, no matter how many times it's washed.

Our lives are topsy-turvy and we feel like foreigners. Did anyone ask us if we wanted to create a new normal? The benefits are a little murky right now, but change can be good.

Change...

Helps us grow. Most of us are like the plant on my porch whose roots no longer have room to grow. Changing her container will provide the space she needs to expand and thrive.

Reveals our strengths. We are stronger than we think we are. Intense testing shows us that with Holy Spirit power we can do what needs to be done.

Opens up new opportunities. We tend to stay nestled comfortably in routine. When that comfort zone is removed, God opens our eyes to new prospects.

Makes us more compassionate. Our hearts are tender toward those who walk difficult roads. Change deepens our understanding so we can offer grace more freely. We get it.

Growth happens in ground watered by tears. God can use the hurt you feel now to put you in a growth spurt!

Prayer Invitation

Dear God,

The changes in my life have robbed me of normal. I'm uncomfortable. I feel unsure. "Embrace a new normal," they say. What does that look like for me?

Your Word declares all that can be shaken will be shaken until only what can't be shaken remains. (Hebrews 12:27) I'm looking around to see what still stands because my heart quivers.

You, Lord, are my firm foundation. (Matthew 7:24-25) Nothing separates me from Your love. (Romans 8:38-39) When the way is unclear, I know You will light my path. (Psalm 119:105) I trust You, Lord.

In the mighty name of Jesus. Amen.

Pray and ponder

When Your Words Return:

How might embracing your new normal help you grow more like Jesus?

Today, I am grateful for:

Scripture Affirmation:

I rejoice in confident hope. I am patient in my troubles. I pray continuously.
(Romans 12:12)

Hope-filled Declaration:

God is your firm foundation.

Each time we rise,
our capacity increases.
Our wells get deeper,
making more room for
the living waters
of the Holy Spirit.

~ Lisa Bevere

Twenty-One - Forgiveness After Betrayal

Do all that you can to live at peace with everyone. Romans 12:18

Can there be forgiveness after betrayal? Is love strong enough to withstand unfaithfulness? Jesus paints a beautiful picture of reconciliation when He encountered Simon Peter after His resurrection.

Peter was in Jesus' inner circle of three. He boldly proclaimed his love for Jesus and declared he was ready to die alongside Him. (John 13:37) Jesus had changed his name from Simon to Cephas (Peter-Rock). (John 1:42) Yet, Peter betrayed his friend.

As we look closely at this example of disloyalty, what truths can we learn from Jesus and Peter about forgiving betrayal? (John 21)

Restoration depends on the willingness of everyone involved.

Jesus and Peter were open to and eager for reconciliation. It takes the willingness of both parties for restoration to happen.

Peter was willing to answer Jesus' hard questions about their relationship. The betrayer must be open and honest in answering questions, sharing their feelings, and listening to the concerns of the one who has been betrayed. An atmosphere of openness must be established.

Jesus allowed Peter the opportunity to show his sincerity. Jesus sees into the heart of man, we cannot. With proper boundaries in place, we allow them the opportunity to show us by their actions they are serious about change.

Jesus and Peter made plans for their future together. Communication is the foundation of all solid relationships. By discussing their future, Jesus showed His willingness to restore Peter and forgive His betrayal.

Betrayal leaves deep wounds and reconciliation is not always possible. Regardless of whether our relationships are restored or we move forward alone, healing is available to everyone.

Prayer Invitation

Jehovah Rapha,

I have been betrayed. I feel disrespected and humiliated. Trust has been lost and my love damaged. Can this relationship ever be restored? Right now, this seems impossible to me.

Jehovah Rapha, I believe You heal relationship just as You do our bodies. I commit to seeking reconciliation. (Colossians 3:13) I will do all I can to live in peace. Give me wisdom and help me set sound boundaries. (Matthew 7: 16-20) Heal my damaged heart. Please help me to remember I didn't earn the forgiveness You freely gave to me; I must not put a price on the forgiveness I give others. (Ephesians 2:8-9)

In the mighty name of Jesus. Amen.

Pray and ponder

When Your Words Return:

Are your scars a reminder of your healing or of your pain? Journal your thoughts on how to change your perspective.

_____
_____
_____
_____
_____
_____

Today, I am grateful for:

_____
_____
_____
_____

Scripture Affirmation:

I trust God. He never lies or changes His mind. He keeps all His promises.
(Numbers 23:19)

Hope-filled Declaration:

The scars on your heart are evidence of God's healing.

Twenty-Two - Bewildered by Circumstances

For God is not a God of disorder but of peace,... 1 Corinthians 14:33

The person who first used the word, discombobulation, must have felt bewildered by their circumstances. It's a back and forth feeling. Yesterday, we felt steady. Today, we feel unsure. Tomorrow will be something entirely different.

When our lives have been disturbed, we seek order. When we can't find it, we want to run from the situation and return when every little thing has once again settled in its proper place.

Life doesn't work that way, does it?

Satan lies to us and tells us we will never have peace and contentment again. It's easy to believe him because discouragement seeps in and catches us off guard.

The truth is life will not always feel turned upside down. God is a God of order and He will help restore it in our lives. Perfection is not realistic but contentment is available. The Apostle Paul tells us we can be content in whatever situation we face, "...for I have learned to be content with whatever I have." (Philippians 4:11)

I once told my counselor, Gil, I felt like I would never handle my emotions in a healthy way. He asked, "Are you handling them better today than last month? How about last year?" When I looked at my life from that perspective, I could see growth and change.

Moving from chaos to contentment is a process. We often extend grace to others, why not give it to ourselves as we wait for God to restore peace and order in our lives?

Prayer Invitation

Abba Father,

Some days are better than others. One day I feel strong; the next day I feel unsure of my future. On the weariest of days, I feel like I haven't grown one bit emotionally. Open my eyes, Lord, to the improvement You are working in my heart. (Philippians 1:6)

Help me to offer myself the gift of grace. I don't need to be perfect. (2 Corinthians 12:9) Thank You, Daddy God, for leading me gently toward wholeness and health.

In the mighty name of Jesus. Amen.

Pray and ponder

When your Words Return:

Are you stronger today than you were last year, last month, or last week? Name one way you have changed for the better.

_____

_____

_____

_____

_____

_____

Today, I am grateful for:

_____

_____

_____

_____

Scripture Affirmation:

My faith in Jesus has made me a new person. My old life is gone and my new life has begun. 2 Corinthians 5:17

Hope-filled Declaration:

God empowers you to handle difficulties differently now.

Twenty-three – Recalculating the Route

Only I can tell you the future before it even happens. Everything I plan will come to pass, for I do whatever I wish. Isaiah 46:10

Do you ever feel as if you have taken the wrong exit off the freeway of life?

I do.

I look up and think, *where am I and how did I get here?* We travel along on cruise control and then trouble darts into the path like a scared deer forcing us to recalculate the route.

Our life paths are filled with recalculations.

The road we travel today is a change from the originally planned route. This new path is a little hilly and curvy. Some days we see mountains ahead. On others, flat terrain is a welcome relief.

The feelings that make us want to return to our usual course are natural. We want familiar but familiar seems so far behind us now. We become fearful of what's next.

This fear of the unknown can bring us to a standstill during recalculations. The temptation is to cease forward movement until we have assurances of what the future holds. God promises light to guide our feet not a flood light for the entire journey. (Psalm 119:105)

Can we trust God to direct our steps toward our next destination? He knows the way even when we can't see what's around a curve or over the hill.

Just as we trust the painted lines on a highway to keep us in the correct lane and moving in the proper direction, we can trust God to steer our lives when we are unsure. He provides everything we need no matter how many times life's troubles cause us to recalculate our routes.

Prayer Invitation

Heavenly Father,

I'm feeling unsettled today. I need direction and wisdom. Your Word promises You give wisdom freely to all who ask. (James 1:5) Well, I'm asking.

I don't like this one bit. I'm walking it, but I'm walking slowly, unsure of my new route. My mind keeps wondering where You were when life hit me and knocked me onto the next road? Open my eyes to Your nearness. (Psalm 145:18)

I am thankful for Your patience. I don't sound like I trust Your care and provision, but I do. I really do. Help me to trust you more. I love You, Lord.

In the mighty name of Jesus. Amen.

Pray and ponder

When your Words Return:

Without knowing every turn of your recalculated route, what is the next step in your journey?

_____

_____

_____

_____

_____

_____

Today, I am grateful for:

_____

_____

_____

_____

_____

Scripture Affirmation:

My ears hear Your direction, Lord. You tell me to go right or left. (Isaiah 30:21)

Hope-filled Declaration:

God fills your new path with hope.

Twenty-four- Hiding the Hurt

O my people, trust in him at all times. Pour out your heart to him, for God is our refuge. Psalm 62:8

Within each of our hearts, there are places we leave untouched — veiled. Maybe those places seem too dark or they are too painful. Our hurt boxes resemble nesting boxes — a big box of hurt that contains several small boxes holding the specifics of a painful event.

We smile, go to work, take care of our families, attend church, and ferociously guard these secret places that weight heavy on our souls.

What do we do with these little sacred boxes? If we open them, we will need to process the feelings we have hidden. If we ignore them, we can pretend we don't know they exist.

The thing about ignoring our pain is that time alone doesn't heal our wounds. We might suppress feelings, but they linger within and cause stress.

In God's patience and wisdom, He gently exposes the places He wants to restore. Processing our feelings and emotions is hard work. The kind that sometimes gets worse before it feels better. I know because I have asked God to mend deep hurts within my heart and it was painful. His love gives us the courage to move forward.

The truth is our hurt boxes have always been transparent to God. He is El Roi, the God Who Sees us. He sees through the veil we try to hide our hurts behind.

But He waits patiently, tenderly encouraging us to invite Him to help us unveil those hurts so He can bring healing. Transparency with God might not feel like a party, but it can be a celebration.

Prayer Invitation

El Roi,

I have memories of painful times stored deep within my heart. Hurt boxes that hide unhealed old wounds. How can I open those boxes to Your healing, Lord? Who, better than You, knows how to turn my mourning into dancing? (Psalm 30:11)

Guide me, Lord, as I unwrap painful times. I'm ready to begin releasing my hurt and resentment to You. I give You my fear and I receive Your healing.

Restore me, Lord!

In the mighty name of Jesus. Amen.

Pray and ponder

When Your Words Return:

If you approached your hidden hurts with godly courage, how could your life change?

_____

_____

_____

_____

_____

_____

Today, I am thankful for:

_____

_____

_____

_____

_____

Scripture Affirmation:

The Lord rescues me from my troubles. (Psalm 34:19)

Hope-filled Declaration:

Christ's healing power is making your heart whole and well.

Twenty-Five – Weathering Sudden Storms

He stilled the storms to a whisper;
the waves of the sea hushed. Psalm 107:29 NLT

Every time I look at the ocean, I remember the greatness of God Almighty. The waves I love to hear lapping the shore can quickly change to white caps crashing into the beach with a deafening sound. Reminds me of life.

It can be beautiful, peaceful, and full of opportunities, yet also dark, unsettled, and filled with unknowns. What do we do when we feel like a little dinghy in the middle of the sea?

The disciples' experience with a sudden storm teaches us some timeless truths about life's squalls. Terror-struck as high waves filled their boat, they cried out to their sleeping Savior. Jesus awoke and silenced the wind and waves, but He also gently rebuked the disciples, citing a lack of faith as the source of their fears. (Mark 4:37-41) Jesus calmed the seas, but not the disciples' hearts. Like us, they were still learning about the power of Jesus' words.

Here are my four takeaways from this story:

1) Our relationship with Jesus does not prevent a sudden tempest.
2) The fear of drowning distorts our perception of our position and provision.
3) No storm in our lives is out of God's control.
4) Jesus may be quiet but He is not unaware.

As we ride out our storms, security comes with the knowledge that God is riding it out with us. The more we watch Him work, the more we learn about His character. In the process of calming the whirlwind around us, our faith grows.

Prayer Invitation

Help, Lord!

I am in a storm! I didn't expect it and now I feel as if I am drowning, unable to speak as waves crash over my head. Please whisper calm over the waves of despair that threaten to overtake me, Lord. (Mark 4:39) Your Word is my life preserver keeping me afloat and bringing me to safety.

I will live and tell of others of how You saved me. (Psalm 71:15)

In the mighty name of Jesus. Amen.

Pray and ponder

When your words return:

In retrospect, what is the most powerful life lesson God taught you during a difficult time in your life?

Today, I am grateful for:

Scripture Affirmation:

The storms of life will not overtake me. I will pass through my fiery trial and not be burned. (Isaiah 43:2)

Hope-filled Declaration:

The Master of the wind pilots your lifeboat.

My deepest
desperation
can lead to a
great revelation
from God.

~ Lysa TerKeurst

Twenty-six - Using Hurt for God's Glory

Come and listen, all you who fear God, and I will tell you what he did for me.
Psalm 66:16

One of those toad strangling rains was coming. Sheets of water made it almost impossible to see. The road we traveled had no shoulders. There was no place to pull off and wait for the storm to pass. Up ahead, we saw a tiny speck of red — car tail lights moving cautiously forward. *If we can follow those lights, we can make it to safety.*

When the rains of adversity fall, we need someone a little further down the road to guide us along the way. One of the ways we can process our hurt is to look for someone a little farther back on the path and offer them encouragement, "Share each other's burdens, and in this way obey the law of Christ." (Galatians 6:2)

In his letter to the Philippian church, the Apostle Paul spoke of being poured out like a drink offering for them (2:17). When we comfort others in our trouble, we sacrifice our desire to hide our brokenness and make a love offering to those in need. We become Jesus with skin on to those around us.

The reason for some of our pain will be apparent. But we will not understand other wounds this side of eternity. We will experience heartbreaks that require the glorified eyes of heaven to comprehend. We can begin overcoming difficult times by using our testimony to bring hope to the hurting.

The testimony of how God comforted us has great value to those He places in our path. Pointing others to the Great Comforter always brings Him glory.

Prayer Invitation

Heavenly Father,

Others with broken hearts have found their way into my life. The Apostle John shares that one way to overcome in the spiritual battle we fight is by the word of our testimony (Revelation 12:11)

Without You, God, my pain would never be used for anything good. I offer my hurt to You as a sacrifice of praise. (Hebrews 13:15) Strengthen me to open my mouth and tell of Your miraculous work in me. Someone needs my story. Place them in my path and give me the words to say to comfort them with the comfort You have given me.

In the mighty name of Jesus. Amen.

Pray and Ponder

When your words return:

Who can you comfort with your testimony?

_____

_____

_____

_____

_____

_____

Today, I am grateful for:

_____

_____

_____

_____

_____

_____

Scripture Affirmation:

I am kind and compassionate to others. (Ephesians 4:32)

Hope-filled Declaration:

God can use your hurt to comfort those hurting around you.

Twenty-seven - Change Them, Lord

For we are each responsible for our own conduct.
Galatians 6:5

We embrace change, as long as the change happens in the lives of other people. The beam in our eye usually hides our weaknesses. (Matthew 7:5)

Our hurting hearts' prayers focus on God changing the one who has hurt us, and when God isn't moving quickly enough to shake some sense into them, we take on the project ourselves. Believing we can affect change in someone else is a lie from Satan. It sets us up for frustration and disappointment.

A healthy mindset grasps this truth — we cannot change anyone but ourselves. As we process our pain, we begin to see God's focus — "Prayer changes things, but it ultimately changes the one who prays."[xiii]

Through our relationship with Him, we learn to adjust our focus to becoming more and more like Jesus and less like someone waiting on others to make us feel better. Our happiness is our responsibility.

We become disappointed when we hand our happiness over to others. People can never meet all our expectations. Each of us has let someone down.

As we seek God, He creates a climate within and around us to promote our development. He promises to work within us to give us the desire and the power to please Him. (Philippians 2:13)

I often speak life over women by saying, "Become the healthiest you possible — spiritually, physically, and emotionally. Let God handle everyone else."

Prayer Invitation

Dear Lord,

I have prayed so many times for others to change. Over and over my heart pleads for understanding and help.

Slowly You, Lord, are beginning to help me see how I need to change. This awareness is hard. My heart is tender. (2 Corinthians 5:17) Focus my eyes on You and empower me to be the best me I can be.

I am anxious about the changes a new day might bring but I want to be completely healed.

Grow me, Lord, but please be gentle. (Jeremiah 10:24)

In the mighty name of Jesus. Amen.

Pray and ponder

When your words return:

List one hope you have for your future. How might what God is doing through your current circumstances shape that hope?

_____

_____

_____

_____

_____

Today, I am grateful for:

_____

_____

_____

_____

_____

Scripture Affirmation:

God is doing a new thing within me. Springs of joy are bubbling up in every dry place in my life. (Isaiah 43:19)

Hope-filled Declaration:

God surrounds you with new opportunities.

Twenty-eight - The Barrier of Self-sufficiency

It was a beautiful thing that you came alongside me in my troubles.
Philippians 4:14 MSG

Life is sweeter with friends. They share in our troubles, laugh with us, cry with us, get mad with us, and hold our hands while we mourn. In a world with an emphasis on social media and virtual friends, true – in real life - friendship is a blessing.

So, why do we resist their help when we are in pain?

When we are hurt, sometimes our natural response is to withdraw. Being alone with our thoughts has its place in processing our pain, but we also need the comfort of our buddies.

Erecting a wall of self-sufficiency places a barrier between our hurting hearts and the comfort we desperately need.

At self-sufficiency's core is pride. It relies on the lie that we can do all the work of healing by ourselves. And it feeds on the disingenuous notion that we are better Christians if we appear put together, even when we are falling apart.

The truth is, God created relationships to enrich our lives. Satan's evil plan is isolation. Pulling away from our support system is a warning sign that he is up to his old tricks again. If this is where you find yourself today, reach out and allow someone to be a blessing to you. It will bless them as well.

We will have an opportunity to comfort those who have comforted us. Seasons change and our friends will need us to walk alongside them in their troubles as they have shared ours. The gift of encouragement is powerful. May we receive it gracefully and give it abundantly.

Prayer Invitation

Father God,

I struggle to accept help from others. Lending a helping hand brings me joy but needing a hand makes me feel uncomfortable. I would rather work through this alone, but I am weary. My mind is distracted and I feel vulnerable. Help! (Proverbs 29:23)

I love my friends and I know they love me. If they were struggling, I would want to comfort them in any way I could. Help me to let go of my foolish self-sufficiency and realize that You use people to be Your hands and feet in this world. (2 Corinthians 3:5)

Thank you, Lord, for my friends and family. I am grateful for their help. Open my eyes to ways I can comfort them when they need it. (Galatians 6:2)

In the mighty name of Jesus. Amen.

Pray and Ponder

When your Words Return:

Do you struggle with accepting comfort from your friends and family? List two actions you can take this week to release your self-sufficiency and embrace the support you need.

Today, I am grateful for:

Scripture Affirmation:

My friends are loyal and there to help me in my time of need. (Proverbs 17:17)

Hope-filled Declaration:

God provides the loving support you need.

Twenty-nine - The Power of Perspective

My health may fail, and my spirit may grow weak, but God remains the strength of my heart; he is mine forever. Psalm 73:26

Practically speaking, there are some situations that may not ever change. We cannot control others and we cannot always control what happens to us. What we can control is how we respond. Our circumstances don't have to change for us to feel hopeful.

There is power in our perspective. How we perceive our circumstances influences how we respond to the circumstances and how we respond influences our outcome.

Let's discuss a few ways we can change our perspectives on difficult times.

Complicated seasons may seem to last forever. They don't. This hard season will change. There are things we must go through to be the person God created us to be.

Understanding God can use our sufferings to change us, to make us more like Jesus, gives us the power to persevere through difficult circumstances. When God doesn't reveal His purposes this side of heaven, we must choose to trust Him so we do not lose hope. Enjoy the good seasons and ask God what He is trying to cultivate in us during the hard ones.

Our lives here on earth are not the end of the story. When my mom was given a terminal diagnosis, she set her sights on heaven. She believed her eyes would close on earth and open to see Jesus.

It is an eternal perspective that empowers us to walk through tough times. Heaven awaits us. The weariness of this world is not the end of a Christian's story. The knowledge of this enables us to live with contentment as we face our struggles.

Changing our perspective is an ongoing process. We need Holy Spirit power to look at life from His eternal perspective.

Prayer Invitation

Dear Lord,

I am changing. I feel a shift in my perspective and I no longer feel hopeless. (Romans 15:13)

I see You in the morning as I have the courage to get out of bed. Your joy seeps out in a smile I thought would never return to my lips. My dry pillow testifies to a more restful sleep. (Psalm 4:8)

Thank You for being so faithful to me. I love you, Lord.

In the mighty name of Jesus. Amen.

Pray and ponder

When your Words Return:

What is the first step you need to take to change your perspective on your situation?

_____

_____

_____

_____

_____

Today, I am grateful for:

_____

_____

_____

_____

_____

Scripture Affirmation:

My gaze is not fixed on my troubles, it is fixed on heaven.
(2 Corinthians 4:17-18)

Hope-filled Declaration:

Your eternal hope puts problems into proper perspective.

Thirty – Jesus is Our Peace

Peace I leave with you; my peace I give to you. Not as the world gives do I give to you. Let not your hearts be troubled, neither let them be afraid.
John 14: 27 ESV

In the middle of stress-filled situations, where can we find peace? May I introduce Him to you? Jesus Christ is not only the Peace Maker; He is the Peace Keeper. The Holy Spirit describes Jesus in the book of Isaiah,

"Wonderful Counselor, Mighty God, Everlasting Father, Prince of Peace."
(Isaiah 9:6)

In the most difficult of times, Jesus was calm. With the shouts of angry mobs resounding in His ears, peace protected His heart and mind. (Isaiah 26:3) The peace Jesus gives has been described as "tranquility of the soul."[xiv]

Jesus' peace is dispensed as a gift. The Holy Spirit is the Peace Giver. He is our Advocate and He dispenses Jesus' peace (Galatians 5:22)

Jesus' peace is firmly rooted in relationship. As our trust in Jesus grows, He takes our anxiety and returns peace. We receive the peace *of* God when we have peace *with* God. * (Romans 15:13; 1 Peter 5:7)

Jesus' peace is not of this world. Jesus promises our world will be filled with trouble, but He also promises He has overcome this world. (John 16:33)

Jesus' peace cannot be explained. It is serenity of heart. We feel outwardly distressed yet there is a calmness in our souls. We can only understand this experience in the light of Jesus' presence in our lives. (Philippians 4:7)

With thankfulness we receive Paul's blessing over our lives, "Now may the Lord of peace himself give you his peace at all times and in every situation. The Lord be with you all." (2 Thessalonians 3:16)

Prayer Invitation

Dear Prince of Peace,

In the chaos of my life, Your peace takes over my heart. As I look at my circumstances logically, the calm I feel is illogical. Even through my tears, there is a tranquility within me. (Psalm 23:4) How will I explain this to those who know my situation?

Because You are my Rock, my fortress, the strong tower I hide within, I am more content. (Proverbs 18:10)

Thank you, Lord, for the gift of Your peace. I love You!

In the mighty name of Jesus. Amen.

Pray and ponder

When your Words Return:

Recall a time when you have felt peace in chaos. If you are struggling with finding peace in your situation, write a prayer inviting God to bring you peace and contentment. Use your Pray and Ponder page if you need more space.

Today, I am grateful for:

Scripture Affirmation:

I have peace with God because of Jesus Christ's sacrifice. (Romans 5:1)

Hope-filled Declaration:

God fills your life with peace and contentment.

*If you would like to know more about receiving Jesus Christ as your Savior, a simple salvation prayer is provided in the back of the book.

Thirty-One – Singing A New Song of Hope

He has given me a new song to sing, a hymn of praise to our God. Psalm 40:3a

Each night I struggled to sleep. I knew I needed to rest, but my thoughts refused to allow sleep to take over my body.

Then I remembered reading about David's ability to calm King Saul with music in 1 Samuel 16: 16-23:

> *"Let us find a good musician to play the harp whenever the tormenting spirit troubles you. He will play soothing music, and you will soon be well again."*

When our thoughts torment us, music can calm our hearts. In the early stages of healing, the playlist we need will contain songs that speak of God's healing presence amidst our pain. Mine did.

But as we begin to heal, a natural shift occurs in the songs we sing. Praising God changes us.

Just as music calms our anxious heart, music will help us celebrate our healing. Slowly we notice our playlist changing as hope enters and peace begins to chase sadness away. God gently guides our hearts to trade lamentations for praise and worship.

Praising God changes us. David encourages us to praise God all the time. (Psalm 34:1) Choosing to worship God during our most difficult times testifies to our faith in God's power and goodness. We praise Him even before He answers. "Faith shows the reality of what we hope for; it is the evidence of things we cannot see." (Hebrews 11:1)

By faith, we sing a new song.

"Sing a new song to the Lord! Let the whole earth sing to the Lord!" Psalm 96:1

Prayer Invitation

Abba Father,

I am beginning to hear the faintest notes of a new song in my heart. (Psalm 40:3) A hymn of hope-filled praise to You, my God. When my foot stumbled, Your unfailing love supported me. When doubts filled my mind, Your comfort gave me hope. (Psalm 94:18-19)

When I was sick at heart, Your love was like a healing balm. I will sing of Your love forever. (Psalm 89:1)

In the mighty name of Jesus. Amen.

Pray and Ponder

When Your Words Return:

What is your favorite way to worship God? How might praising God despite your circumstances change your feelings?

_____
_____
_____
_____
_____
_____

Today, I am grateful for:

_____
_____
_____
_____
_____

Scripture Affirmation:

I praise God with singing and honor Him with thanksgiving.
(Psalm 69:30)

Hope-filled Declaration:

Praising God ushers in your healing.

God wants to
bring us healing,
but more than
anything, He wants us
to know our healer.

~ Beth Moore

A Simple Salvation Prayer

ABCs of Salvation:

A – Admit you have sinned. "For everyone has sinned; we all fall short of God's glorious standard." (Romans 3:23)

B – Believe in Jesus. "For this is how God loved the world: He gave his one and only Son, so that everyone who believes in him will not perish but have eternal life." (John 3:16)

C – Confess and leave your sin behind. "But if we confess our sins to him, he is faithful and just to forgive us our sins and to cleanse us from all wickedness." (1 John 1:9)

Lord, I admit that I have done things that are wrong. Thank You that You died to take away all my sins and arose in victory to give me life abundantly. Please forgive me. I receive Your forgiveness now and declare that I want to live for You for the rest of my life. Come and fill me with Your Holy Spirit. I now depend completely on You.

In the mighty name of Jesus. Amen.

Welcome to the family of God! Your next steps are:

1) **Tell somebody how God changed your life**.
2) **Begin reading your Bible. The book of John, in the New Testament, is a great place to start.**
3) **Pray daily. You don't need fancy words. Prayer is talking to God.**
4) **Find a biblically sound local congregation to grow and serve God with the gifts and talents He has given you. If you don't know of one, ask a Christian friend.**

If you prayed this prayer for salvation, I would love for you to drop me a note at carmen@carmenhorne.com and let me rejoice with you!

Notes

Notes

Notes

Meet the Author

Carmen Horne is a Board Certified Advanced Christian Life Coach, writer, speaker, and humorist who uses her gifts to encourage women. She is passionate about supporting women through life's challenges as they learn to draw on God's power and a dynamic relationship with Jesus to change their perspective on the unexpected.

Carmen's father was an alcoholic and she was molested by a friend's dad when she was a child. Healing her own damaged heart taught Carmen the hope she now offers to the brokenhearted. Plowing through unhealthy thinking in her own life shaped Carmen's understanding of the power of perspective. Mentoring, lay counseling, and a listening ear are the original seeds of her ministry.

Carmen is a contributor to *101 Secrets to a Happy Marriage* — Thomas Nelson Publishers, *Warrior Devotional* — Declare Conference, *The Message* and *Just Between Us* magazines, and many online websites and blogs.

At the ripe old age of 16, the Bayou State native married her high-school sweetheart. They recently celebrated their 42nd anniversary and have one beautiful daughter. Carmen is a dark chocolate nibbler and beach sitter. But her favorite activities are those she participates in as a wife and mom.

Connect with Carmen on her website at www.CarmenHorne.com.

Acknowledgements

To my Savior, Jesus Christ, family members, dear friends, and fellow creatives, I offer my heartfelt appreciation:

My Savior and Lord, Jesus Christ. Thank You for saving me, healing me, guiding me, and using me to do Your work. Calling this scared and insecure girl to Your ministry of encouragement astonishes me. I am honored and humbled at the very thought of it. My heart belongs to You forever.

To my sweetheart, Lary. You are my number one cheerleader and offer support in every endeavor. Lary, you are the most generous person I know. Our many years together have grown me in ways I cannot explain, except to say, we are better together. I love you, honey.

Madison, along with Lary and Nana, you are always there to cheer me on. You are a wonderful daughter and friend. From the first day I carried you in my womb, I became compelled to be a better person, for you. Madison, you are my biggest blessing. I love you, sweetie.

Gil Martin. So much of your wisdom is in *Out of Words*. Over and over you have taught me, comforted me, challenged me, and been used by God to heal my broken heart. When we met, 16+ years ago, I had no idea all the twists and turns my life would take. You know my whole story, with all its pretty and ugly places. Lary and I owe you a debt of gratitude that mere words cannot repay. Thank you for allowing God to use you in the healing ministry of Christian counseling. You're are leaving a big legacy, friend.

My ministry prayer team: Betsy Ringer, Carol Keeton, Gil and Pam Martin (my favorite counselor and the only man on the team, besides Lary), Ellen Chauvin, Jana Kennedy-Spicer, Judy Hales, Karen Spruell, Kathleen Dugdale, Kathy Lenard, Kristine Brown, Lisa Townsend, Liz Giertz, Sarah Kelley, Stephanie K. Adams, Sherry Martin, and Tammy Lawless. Your heartfelt prayers and encouragement are invaluable. You prayed me through photo shoots, edits, anxiety attacks, and intense fear. Thank you seems inadequate.

Kim Stewart, Jana Kennedy-Spicer, and Ben Hobson. Thanks for asking me each time we met, "Are you writing a book, yet?" Your encouragement helps me push past fear and procrastination.

Dianne Anders. Thank you for proclaiming in 2011, "You need to write a blog." You planted the first seeds in this journey.

Ellen Chauvin. You listen to me whine, cry and discuss, at length, the ins and outs of writing. Ellen, you are one of the sane voices I call upon when I travel the speculation road. We discuss our inadequacies and our compulsion to write when we don't understand why or how. You are my traveling buddy and my writing buddy. Most of all, you are my dear friend.

My sample readers: Betsy Ringer, Ellen Chauvin, Jana Kennedy-Spicer, Karen Spruell, Kim Stewart, Kristine Brown, Phyllis Horne (a special thank you for all your invaluable advice along the way!), Sabra Penley, Stephanie K. Adams, and Teresa Groce. Thank you for reading my book sample and giving me honest feedback. Your kindness and support gave me encouragement to keep going. It's scary to put our written words out there. Y'all helped calm my fears.

Stephanie K. Adams, Katie Reid, and my hope*writer writing leaders and community. Your expertise has made me be better than I could ever be alone.

Jana Kennedy-Spicer. You dressed my book baby beautifully. Thank you for listening to my many ideas and for helping me, in the end, to narrow down what is really needed. I would never have figured out the formatting process without you. Girl, thank you is not enough.

Liz Giertz. Gosh, your touch was the special sauce on my content. I am a better writer because of your influence. You are editor extraordinaire! The Holy Spirit used both of us to do His work.

Misti Mixon Stone. Your photography skills made my fear of a photo shoot disappear. Thank you for helping me smile a real smile!

Oliva Kemp – Makeup by Oliva. You are truly a professional. Your ability to apply makeup made me feel beautiful.

Additional Resources

Finding Words: Writing from Hurt to Hope

Did you have a diary as a child? Mine is pink with a fairy-sized padlock. Even though the key has long been lost. I still keep it tucked away in the bottom of a drawer. After 45+ years, I still guard its secrets.

Journals are the keepers of our thoughts and feelings. Writing is a wonderful healing experience. Our fingers are our scribes. Taking pen to paper helps us gain an understanding of our experiences. We take note of our feelings as we pour out grief and painful emotions as freely as the ink flows from the pen.

Still, it is often difficult for us to find the words to express the pain we feel. As the ability to voice that pain becomes less strained, our writing will become easier, too.

Releasing feelings through writing is a healthy step toward healing.

In *Finding Words*, the companion journal to her book, *Out of Words*, Carmen provides space to journal your thoughts and prayers. Carefully selected Scriptures mirroring those referenced in her book provide comfort and guidance as you continue your healing journey.

Savor this time with your thoughts and with God. He longs to deepen His relationship with you.

> *"Because he bends down to listen, I will pray as long as I have breath!"*
> *Psalm 116:2, NLT*

For more information and other resources visit:
www.CarmenHorne.com/out-of-words-book/

Out of Words

[i] **From me to you:**
I usually attribute this quote to Clairee Belcher in the movie *Steel Magnolias*. The actual attribution should go to 19th century German philosopher, Friedrich Nietzsche.

Three:
[ii] English translation of a Polish expression: Nie mój cyrk, nie moje małpy

[iii] Anna Bartlett Warner, 1859, Public Domain

[iv] Thurman, Dr. Chris. 1999. *The Lies We Believe*. Nashville, TN: Thomas Nelson. Haper-Collins Christian Publishing, Inc.

[v] Seth J. Gillihan, Ph.D.. *21 Common Reactions to Trauma*, Psychology Today, September 07, 2016, https://www.psychologytoday.com/us/blog/think-act-be/201609/21-common-reactions-trauma (March 29, 2019)

[vi] "Murphy's Law" *Merriam-Webster.com*. https://www.merriam-webster.com/dictionary/Murphy%27s%20Law. (March 29, 2019)

[vii] Lucado, Max. 2017. *Anxious for Nothing: Finding Calm in a Chaotic World*. Nashville, TN: Thomas Nelson. Harper-Collins Christian Publishing, Inc.

[viii] Mayo Clinic Staff. *Generalized Anxiety Disorder*, mayoclinic.org. October 13, 2017. https://www.mayoclinic.org/diseases-conditions/generalized-anxiety-disorder/symptoms-causes/syc-20360803 (March 29, 2019)

[ix] The Gideons International. Nashville, TN

[x] Words: Charlotte Elliot, 1836, Music: William B. Bradbury, 1849

Twenty-Seven:
[xi] Arthur, Kay. 1995. *My Savior, My Friend: A Daily Devotional*, Eugene, OR: Harvest House Publishers

[xii] Unknown origin. There are several attributions for this quote with varied wording.

[xiii] Eller, Suzanne. 2016. *Come with Me: Discovering the Beauty of Following Where He Leads*. Bloomington, MN: Bethany House Publishers. Baker Publishing Group

Thirty-One:
[xiv] John McArthur. *The Gift of Peace*. 1983, https://www.gty.org/library/articles/P21/the-gift-of-peace (April 18, 2019)

Quote Page Attributions:
Listed in order of appearance.

Mother Teresa of Calcutta. 1995. *The Mother Teresa Reader: A Life for God*. Servant Publications, Inc.

Bevere, Lisa. 2016. *Without Rival: Embrace Your Identity and Purpose in an Age of Confusion and Comparison*. Grand Rapids MI: Revell. Baker Publishing Group

Terkeurst, Lysa. 2018. *It's Not Supposed to Be This Way: Finding Unexpected Strength When Disappointments Leave You Shattered*. Nashville, TN: Nelson Books. Harper-Collins Christian Publishing, Inc.

Moore, Beth. 2009. *Praying God's Word: Breaking Free from Spiritual Strongholds*. Nashville, TN: B&H Publishing Group